ALFRED's
ACRED PERFORMER
DUETS

What Can We Play Today?

B͟ices

6 Easily Prepared Piano Duet Arrangements

Arranged by Robert D. Vandall

While in our teens and before we met at college, my wife and I played the piano in our churches. We have continued playing in church as soloists and duettists since we graduated and married. We especially look for sacred duets, which allow us to perform as partners for church services, music club meetings, and recitals.

Each book in this series features hymns, spirituals, and folk tunes that are appropriate for Sundays that fall within two consecutive months of the church year, making planning music around scripture and sermon topics easier. Book 4 is for July and August, and includes selections for the Fourth of July. Other books in this series are as follows:

Book 1: January and February

Book 2: March and April

Book 3: May and June

Book 5: September and October

Book 6: November and December

I hope that performers and congregations will find these arrangements captivating and musically fulfilling.

Robert D. Vandall

Alfred Music Publishing Co., Inc.
P.O. Box 10003
Van Nuys, CA 91410-0003
alfred.com

ISBN-10: 0-7390-8414-3
ISBN-13: 978-0-7390-8414-4

Cover Photo
Window: © stock.xchng.com/beriliu

Battle Hymn of the Republic

SECONDO

American folk song
Arr. Robert D. Vandall

(Approx. Performance Time – 2:45)
The Fourth of July

Battle Hymn of the Republic

PRIMO

American folk song
Arr. Robert D. Vandall

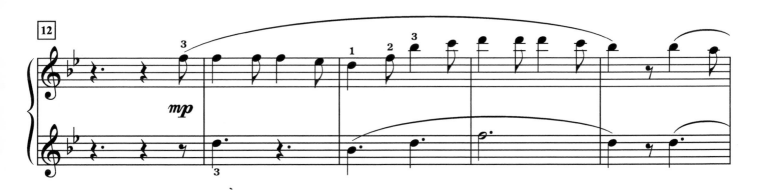

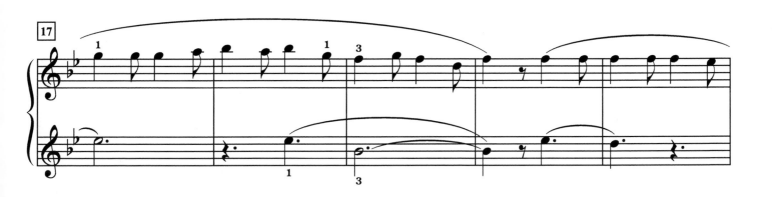

SECONDO

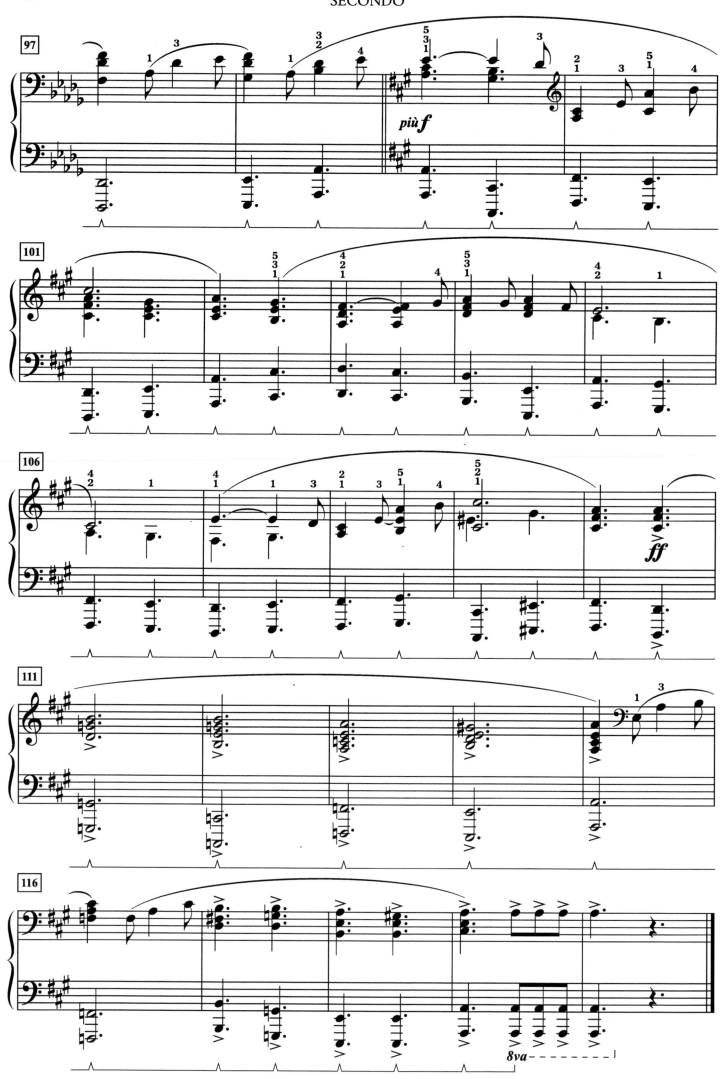

Jesus Loves Me

SECONDO

William B. Bradbury
Arr. Robert D. Vandall

(Approx. Performance Time – 2:15)
General

Jesus Loves Me

PRIMO

William B. Bradbury
Arr. Robert D. Vandall

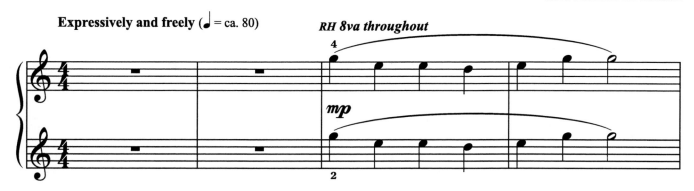

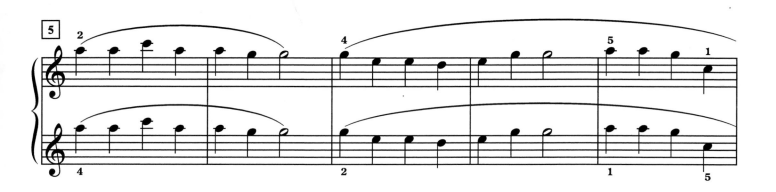

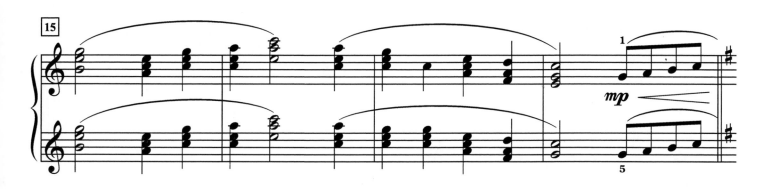

SECONDO

My Country, 'Tis of Thee

SECONDO

Thesaurus Musicus
Arr. Robert D. Vandall

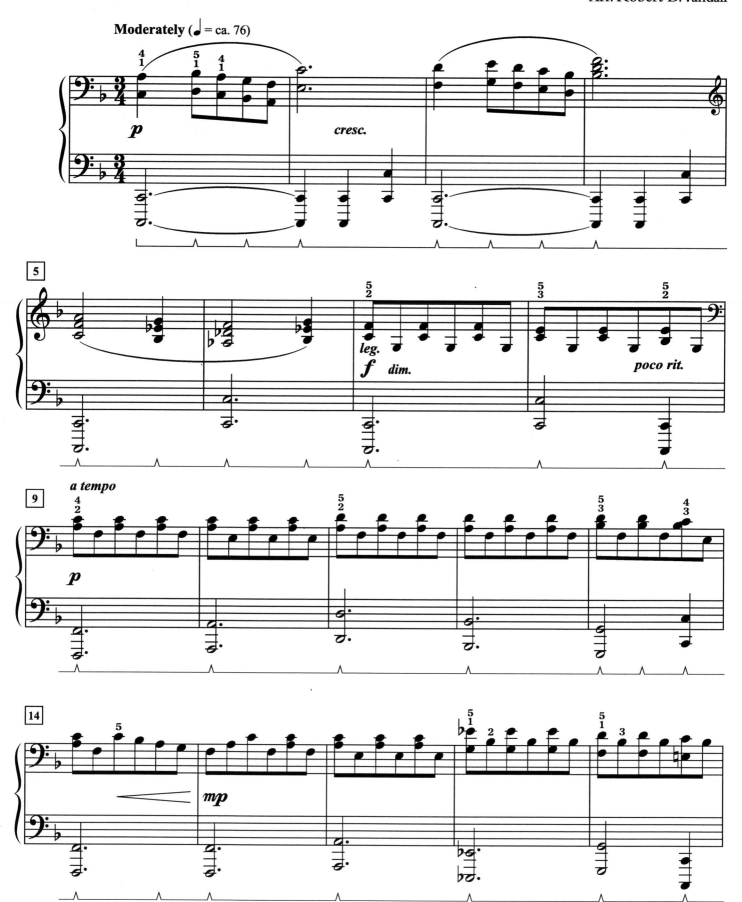

(Approx. Performance Time – 3:30)
The Fourth of July

My Country, 'Tis of Thee

PRIMO

Thesaurus Musicus
Arr. Robert D. Vandall

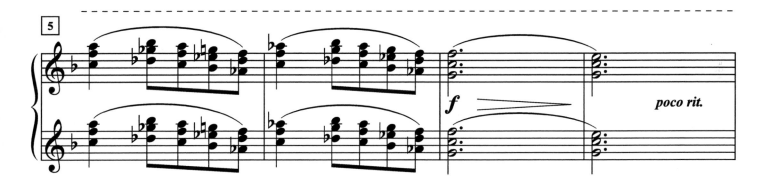

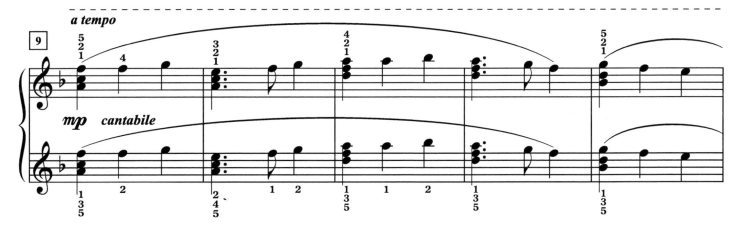

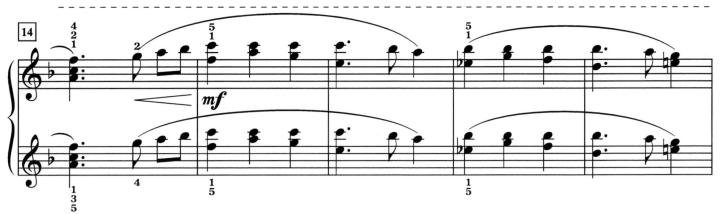

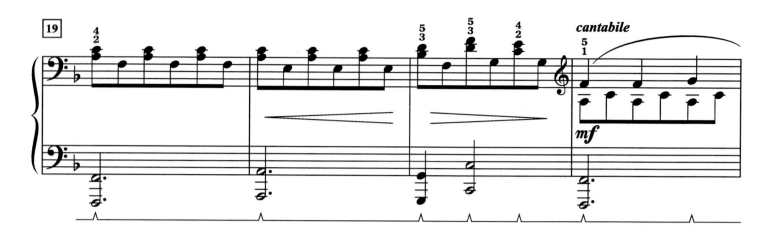

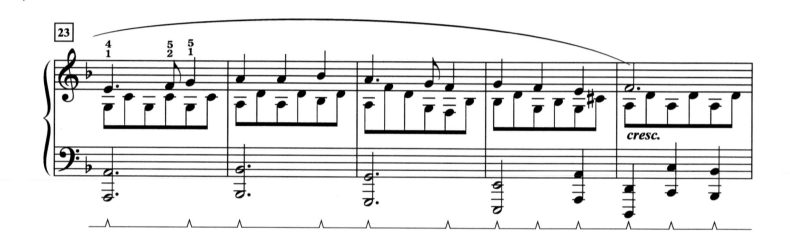

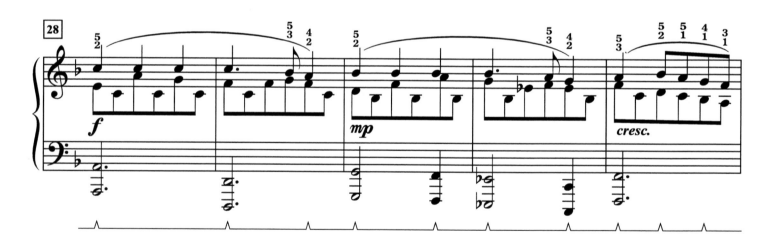

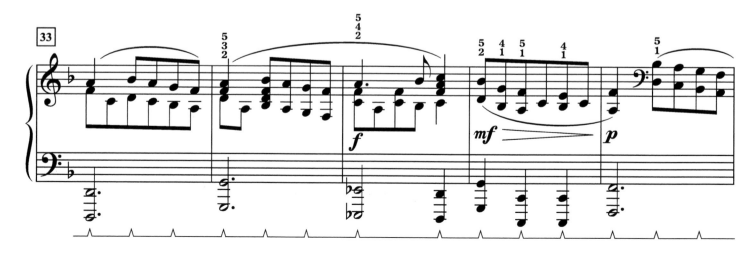

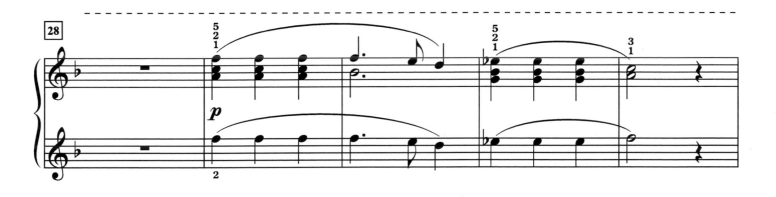

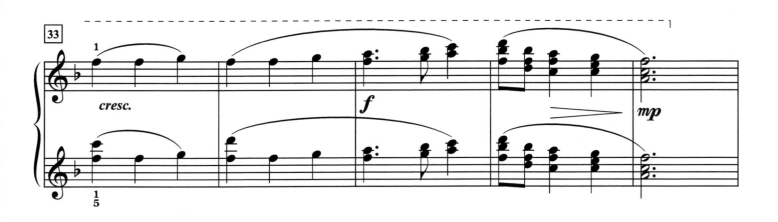

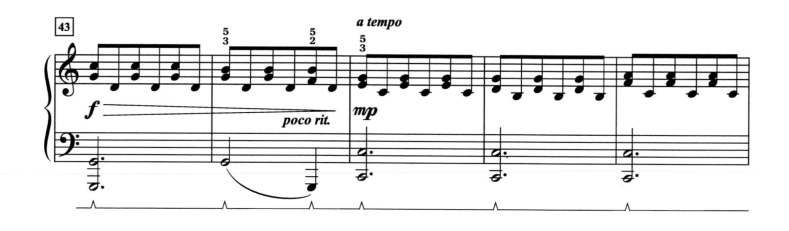

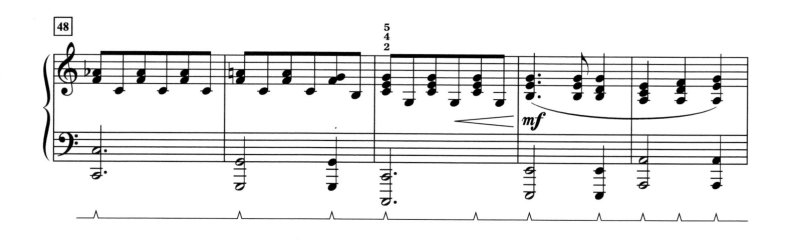

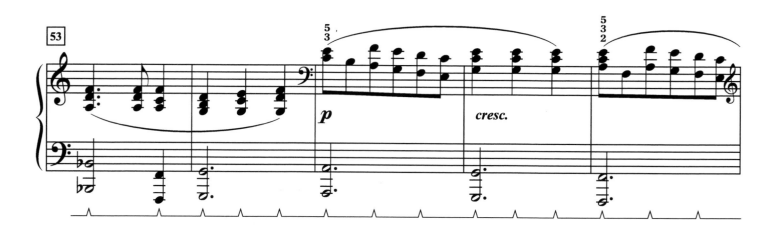

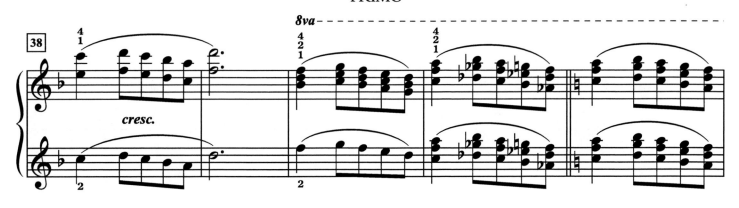

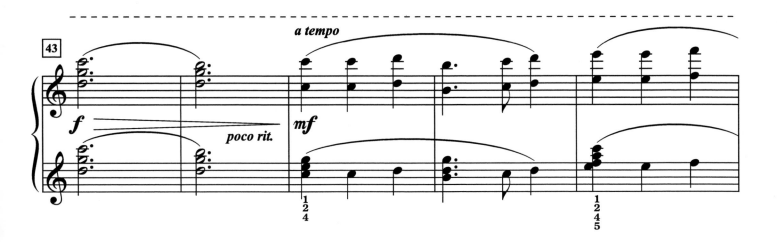

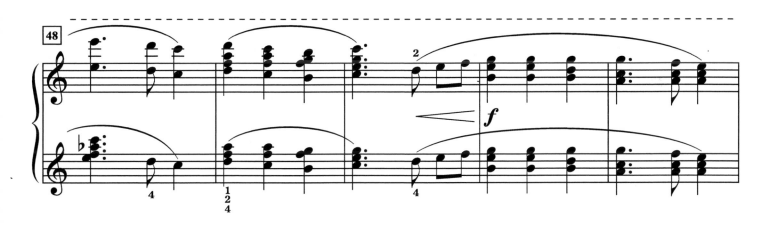

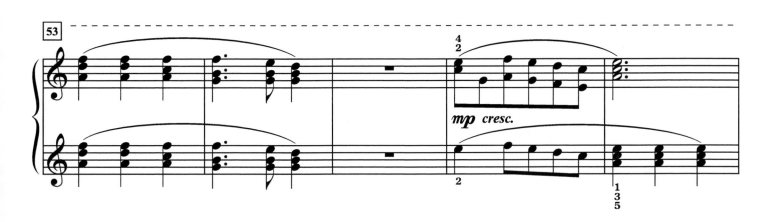

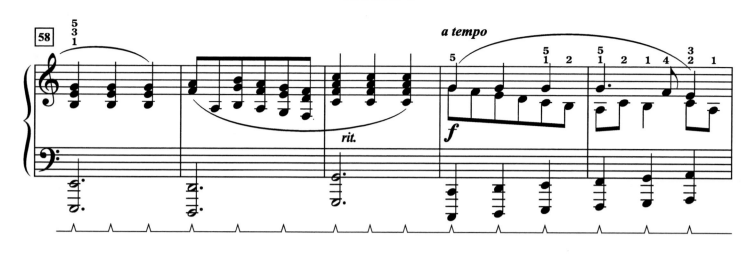

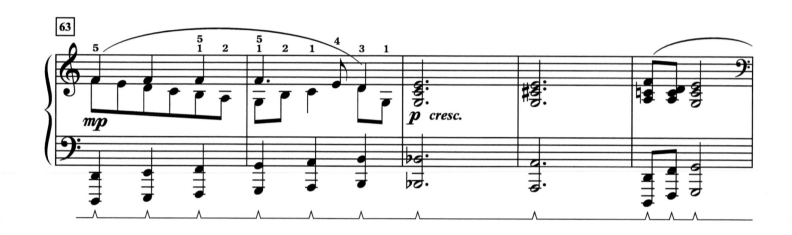

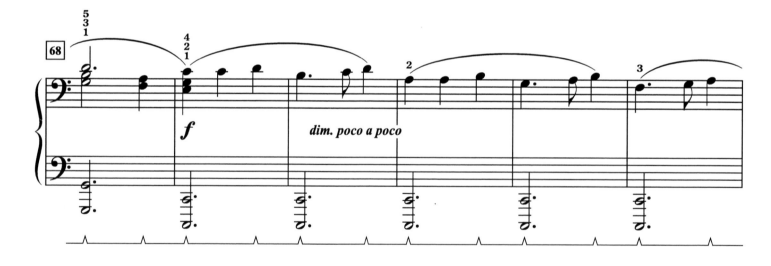

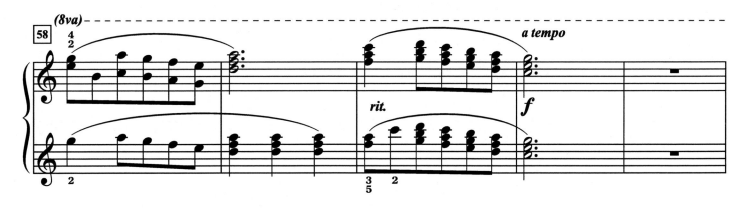

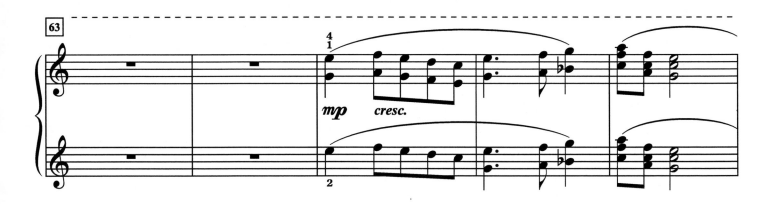

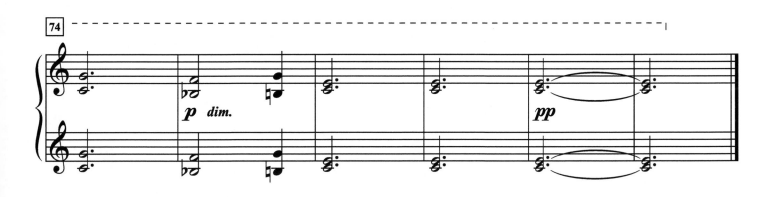

Sweet Hour of Prayer
WITH
Standing in the Need of Prayer

SECONDO

William B. Bradbury/Afro-American spiritual
Arr. Robert D. Vandall

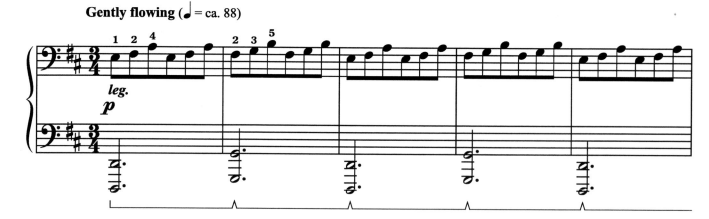

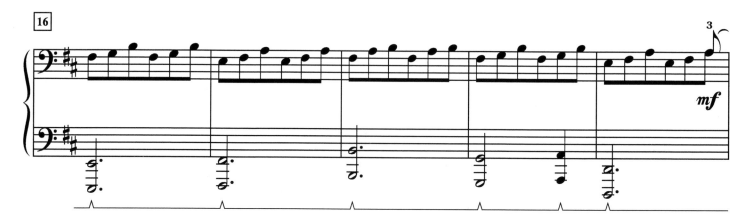

(Approx. Performance Time – 3:00)
General

Sweet Hour of Prayer
WITH
Standing in the Need of Prayer

PRIMO

William B. Bradbury/Afro-American spiritual
Arr. Robert D. Vandall

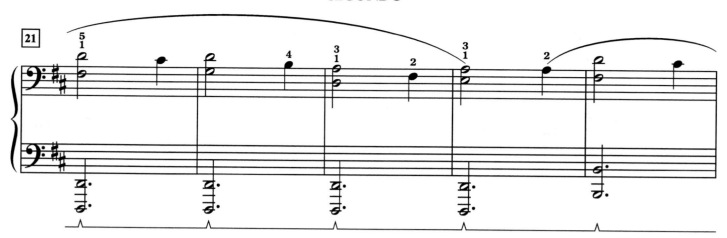

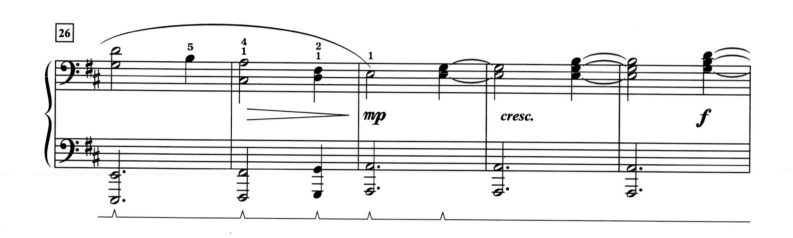

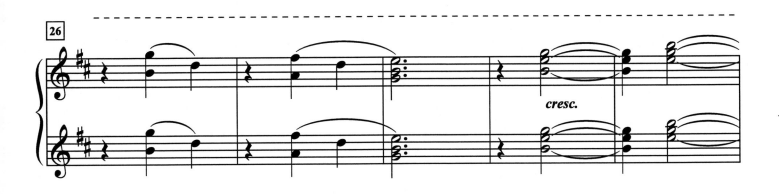

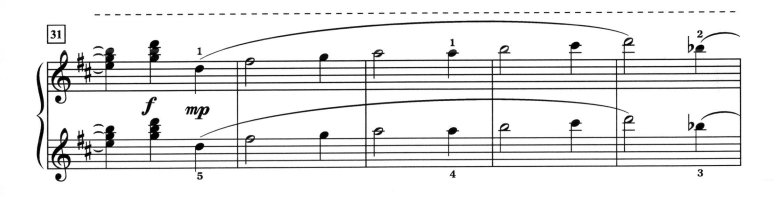

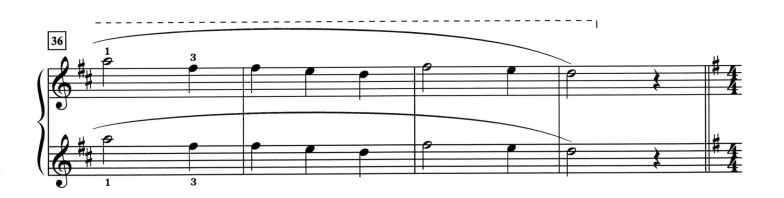

28

SECONDO

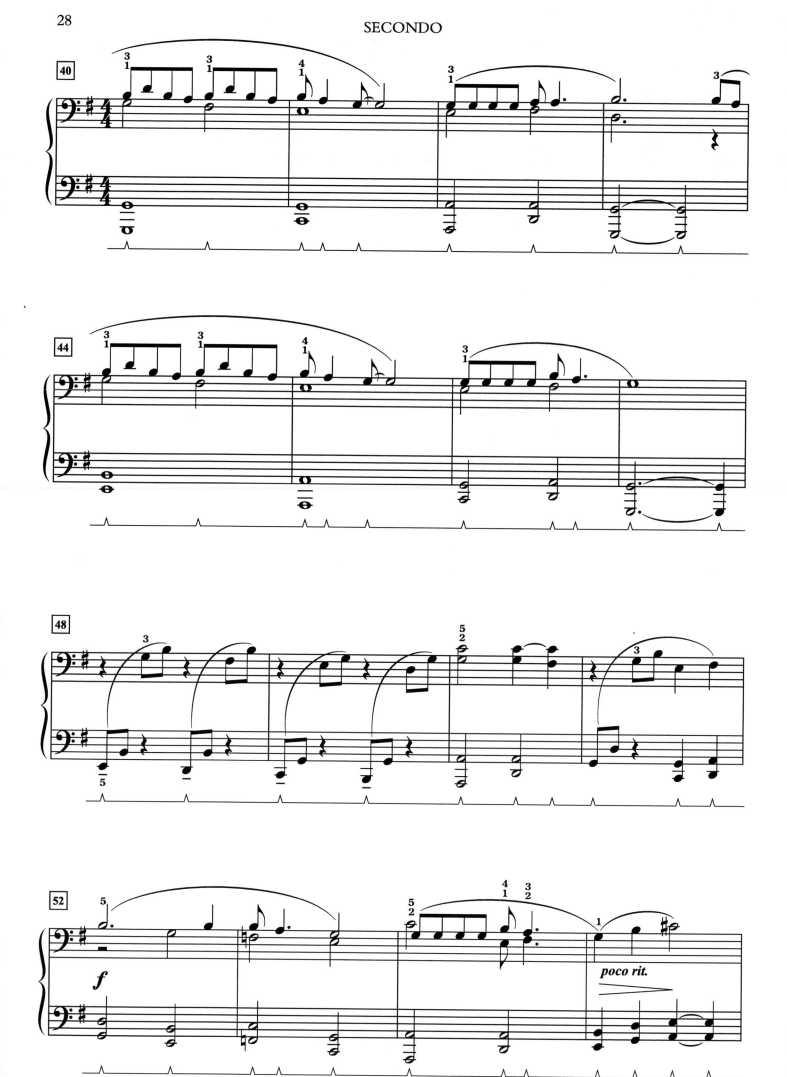

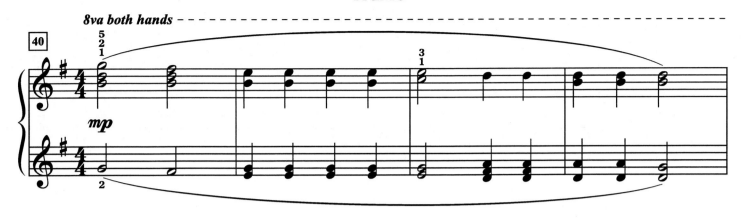

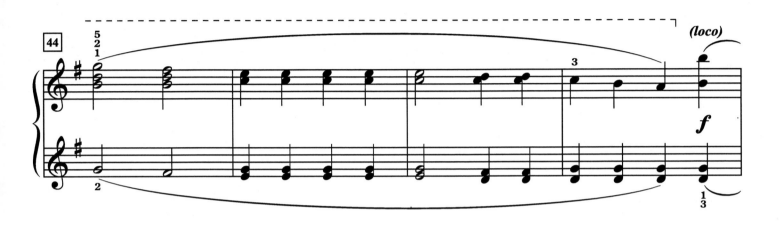

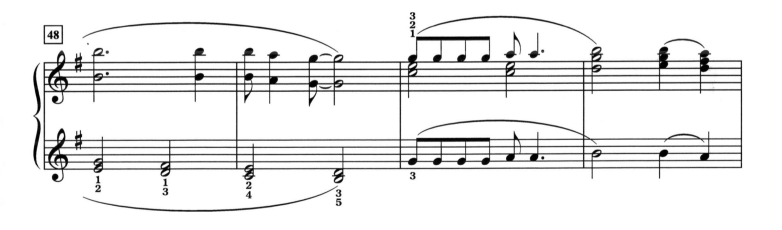

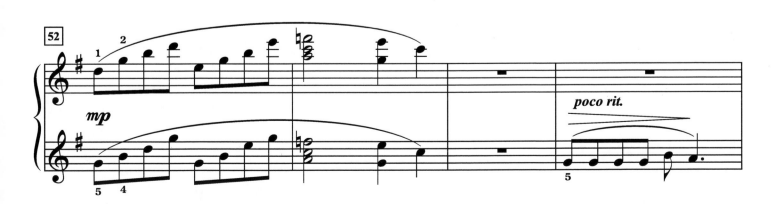

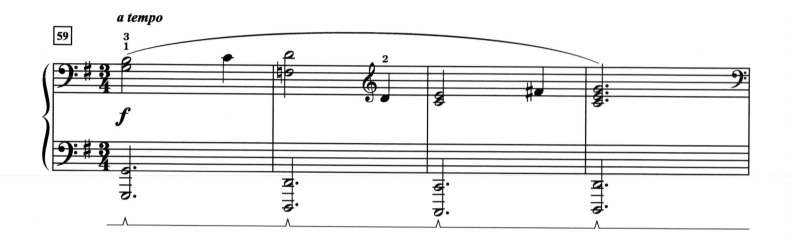

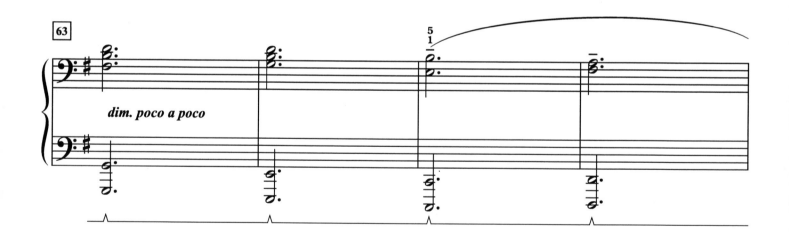

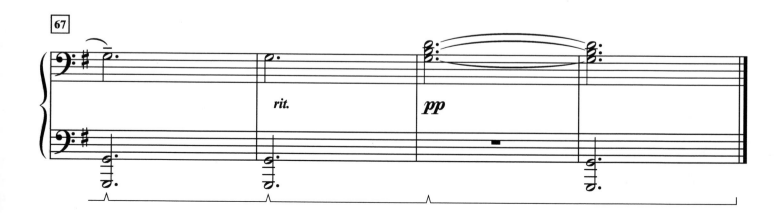

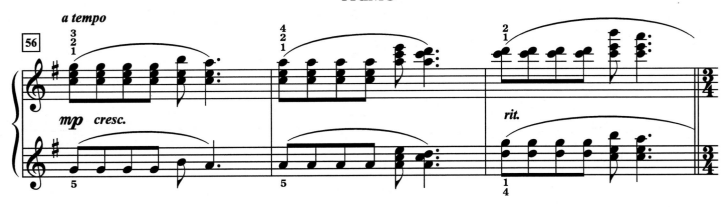

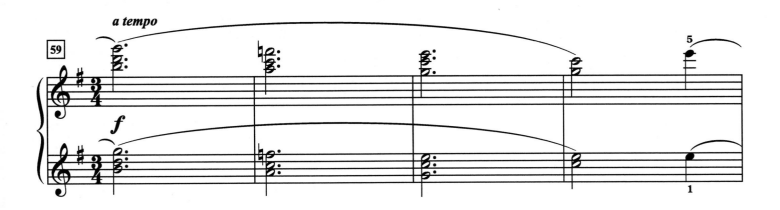

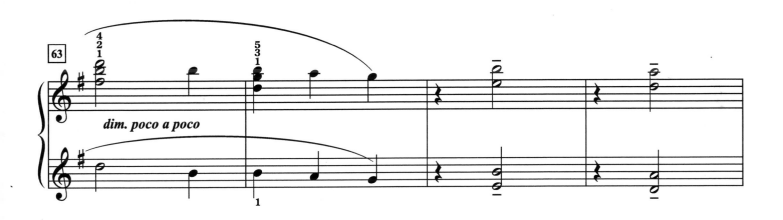

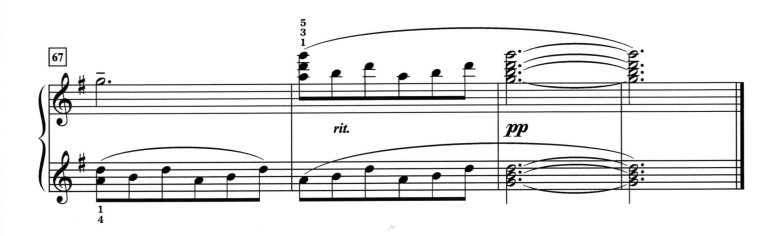

This Is My Father's World

SECONDO

Franklin L. Sheppard
Arr. Robert D. Vandall

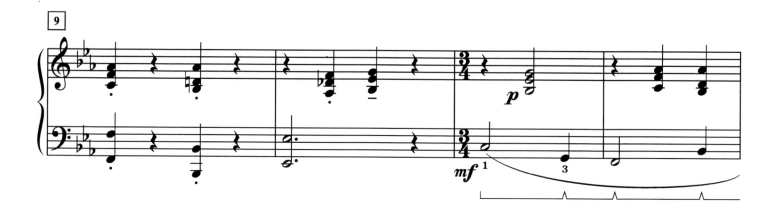

(Approx. Performance Time – 2:00)
General

This Is My Father's World

PRIMO

Franklin L. Sheppard
Arr. Robert D. Vandall

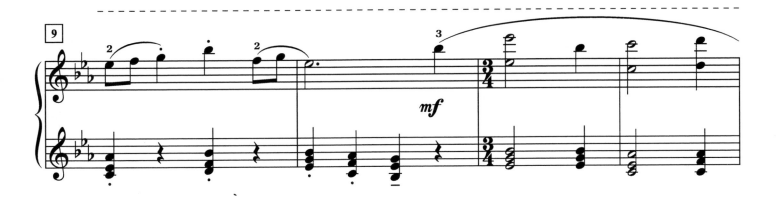

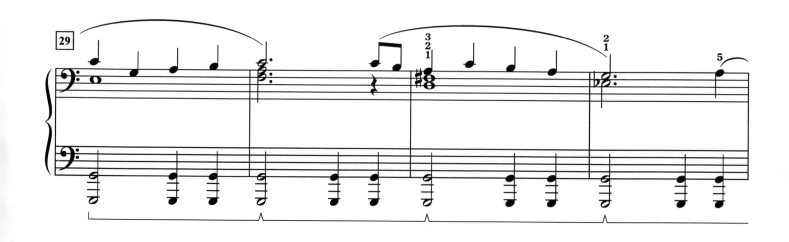

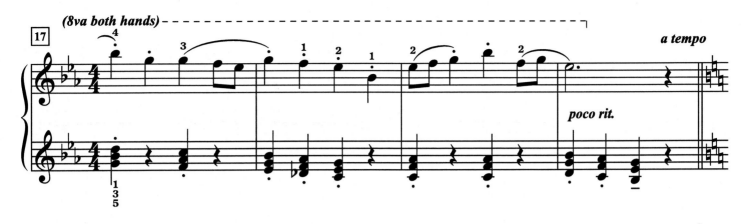

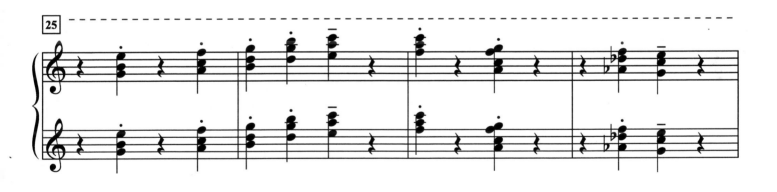

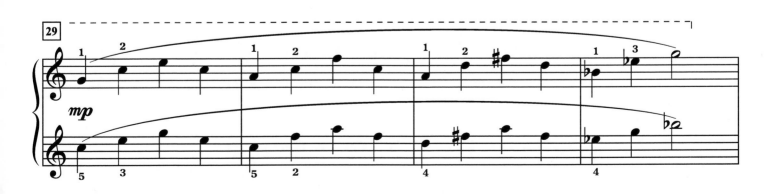

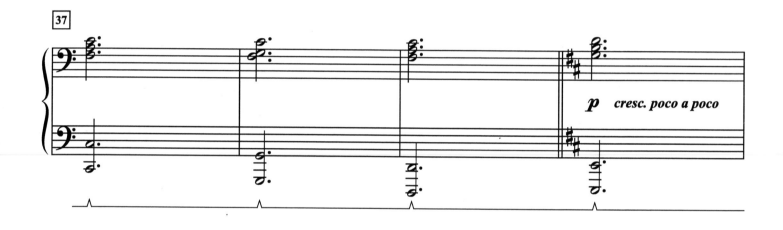

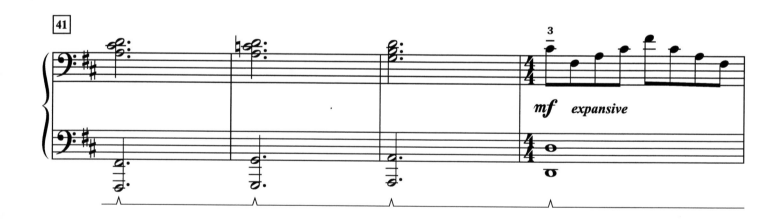

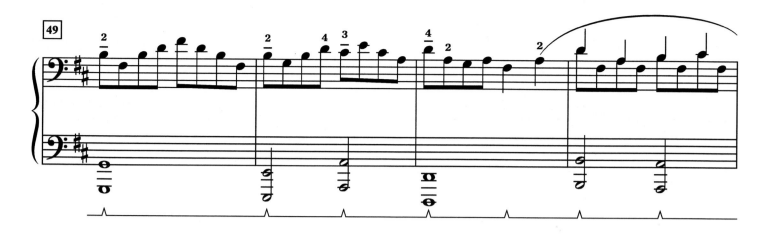

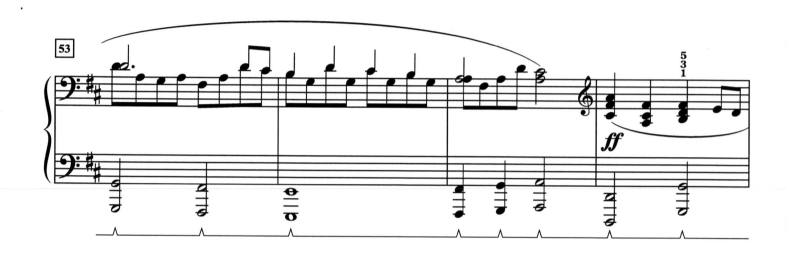

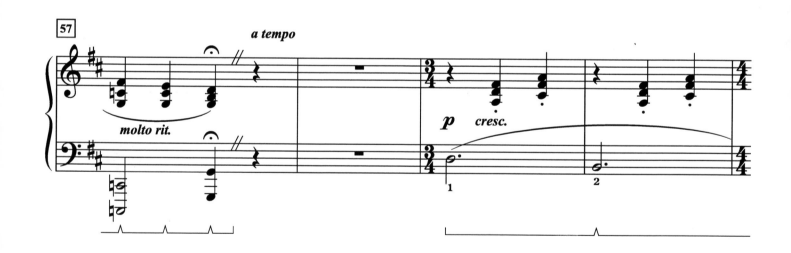

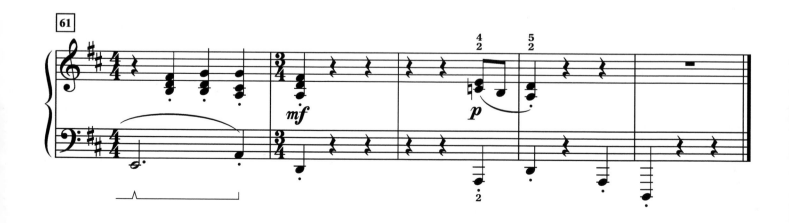

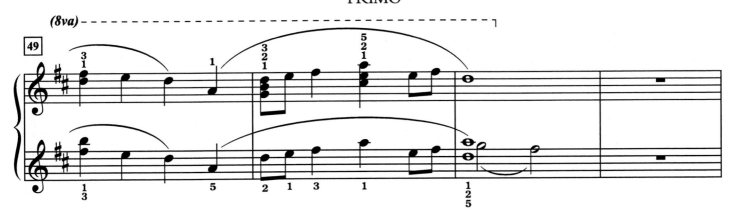

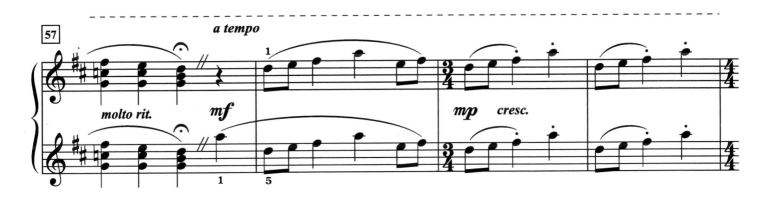

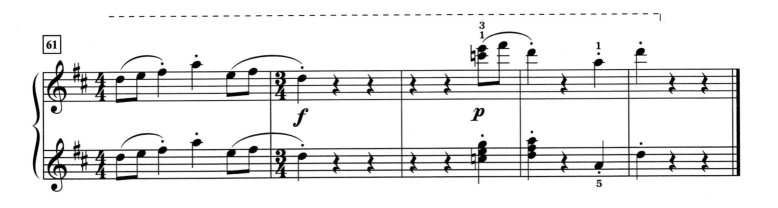

This Little Light of Mine

SECONDO

Afro-American spiritual
Arr. Robert D. Vandall

(Approx. Performance Time – 2:00)
General

This Little Light of Mine

PRIMO

Afro-American spiritual
Arr. Robert D. Vandall

Strongly rhythmic and accented, even eighths ($\quarternote$ = ca. 92)

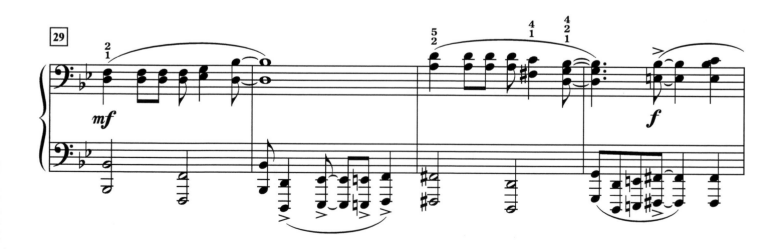

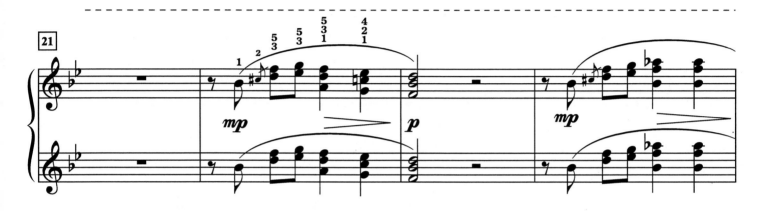

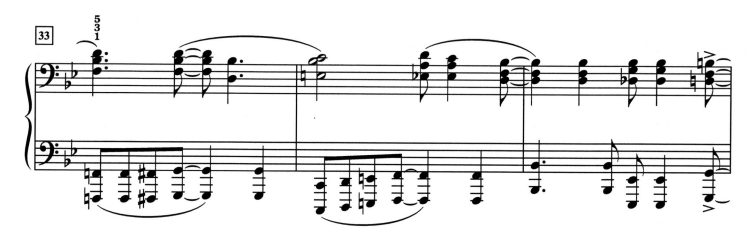

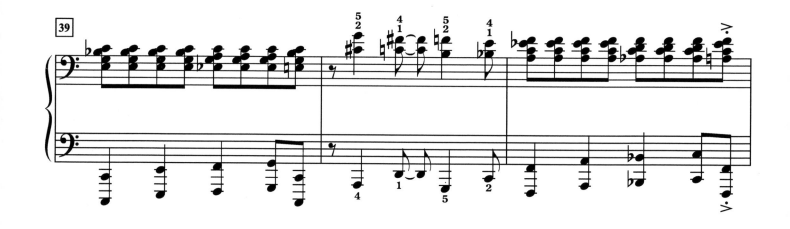

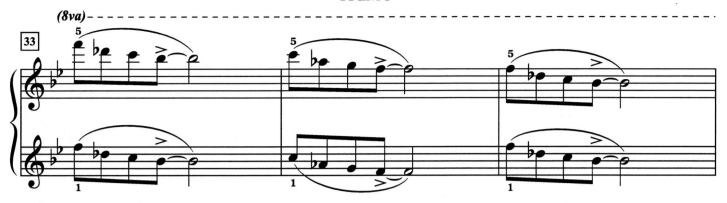

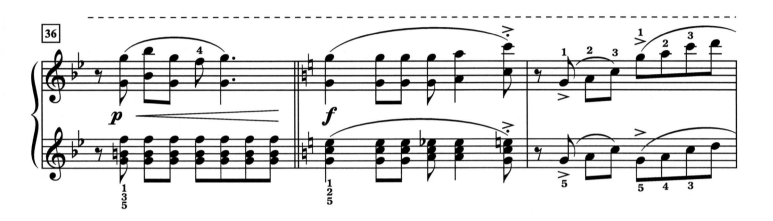

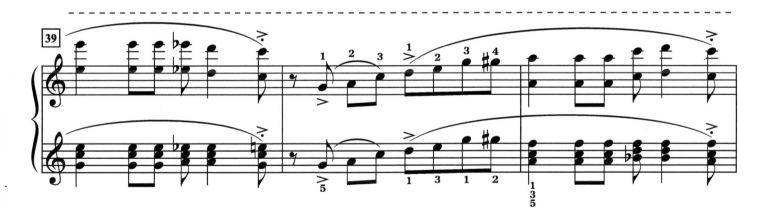

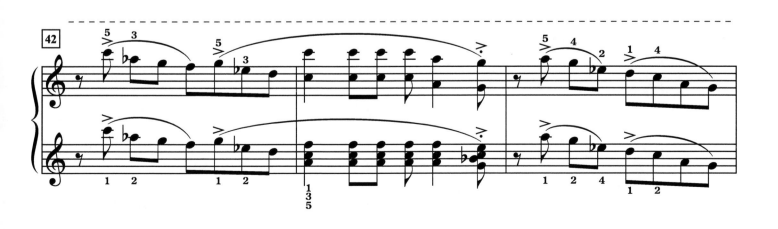

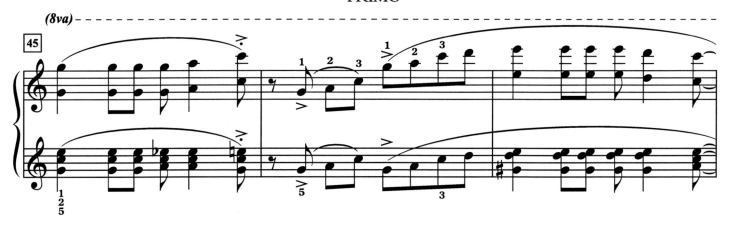

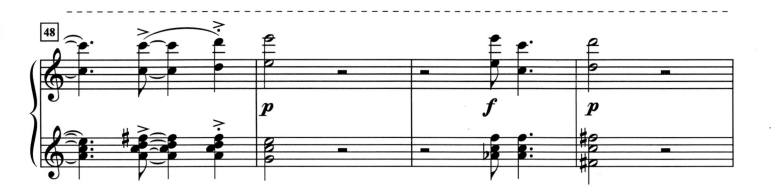

(opt. ad lib. scales,
chords, etc.)